The Satanic Prophet

Book of Lilith

BR Edmunds

I want this book to enlighten you in the way that searching for this enlighten me. Have a good read.

BR Edmunds

Published by:

Kouski Publishing Canada
Ardmore, Ab
Canada

This is the book of Lilith, first wife of Adam and queen of the dammed. I am writing this with the quote, poetry (most my own) and prayers (most my own). This is the second book of the series make sure to checkout "Book of Lucifer" online.

I thank you for supporting me with the purchase of this book and I am putting a lot of work into this series.

There are legends that Adam had a wife before Eve who was named Lilith, but this is not found in the Bible. The legends vary significantly, but they all essentially agree that Lilith left Adam because she did not want to submit to him. According to the legends, Lilith was an evil, wicked woman who committed adultery with Satan and produced a race of evil creatures.

****

Lilith

Lilith is a Jewish Religious figure; she is also in Mesopotamian mythology. Alternatively, the first wife of Adam and supposedly the primordial she-demon. She is citing as to being banished from the Garden of Eden for not complying with and obeying Adam. She is mentioned in biblical Hebrew in the book of Isaiah, and in late antiquity in Mandaean Mythology and Jewish mythology sources from 500 CE onward. Lilith appears as Adam's first wife, who was created at the same time and from the same clay as Adam. Lilith left Adam after she refused to become subservient to him and then would not return to the garden of Eden after she had coupled with the Archangel Samael.

-Wikipedia

Lilith, female demonic figure of Jewish folklore. Her name and personality are thought to be derived from the class of Mesopotamian demons called *lilû* (feminine: *lilītu*), and the name is usually translated as "night monster." A cult associated with Lilith survived among some Jews as late as the 7th century CE. The evil she threatened, especially against children and women in childbirth, was said to be counteracted by the wearing of an amulet bearing the names of certain angels.

In rabbinic literature Lilith is variously depicted as the mother of Adam's demonic offspring following his separation from Eve or as his first wife. Whereas Eve was created from Adam's rib (Genesis 2:22), some accounts hold that Lilith was the woman implied in Genesis 1:27 and was made from the same soil as Adam. Insolently refusing to be subservient to her husband, Lilith left Adam and the perfection of the Garden of Eden; three angels tried in vain to force her return. According to some mythologies, her demonic offspring were sired by an archangel named Samael and were not Adam's progeny. Those children are sometimes identified as incubi and succubi.

-Brittanica

Lilith, a woodcut on paper by Ernst Barlach, *c.* 1922.
Los Angeles County Museum of Art, (The Robert Gore Rifkind Center for German Expressionist Studies;83.1.34.2o), www.lacma.org

Lilith is known to be the first woman to ever be created according to many rabbinic texts (the source of much Jewish mythology). There are several different perspectives of who Lilith is and why she was so dangerous, but all of them involve her hatred towards Adam, Eve, and their descendants.

When God created Adam and saw that he was alone, He created a woman from dust, like him, and named her Lilith. But when God brought her to Adam, they immediately began to fight. Adam wanted her to lie beneath him, but Lilith insisted that he lie below her. When Lilith saw that they would never agree, she uttered God's Name and flew into the air and fled from Adam. Then Adam prayed to his Creator, saying, "Master of the Universe, the woman you gave me has already left me." So God called upon three angels, Senoy, Sansenoy, and Semangelof, to bring her back. God said, "Go and fetch Lilith. If she agrees to go back, fine. If not, bring her back by force."

The angels left at once and caught up with Lilith, who was living in a cave by the Red Sea, in the place where Pharaoh's army would drown. They seized her and said, "Your maker has commanded you to return to your husband at once. If you agree to come with us, fine; if not, we'll drown one hundred of your demonic offspring every day."

Lilith said, "Go ahead. But don't you know that I was created to strangle newborn infants, boys before the eighth day and girls before the twentieth? Let's make a deal. Whenever I see your names on an amulet, I will have no power over that infant." When the angels saw that was the best they would get from her, they agreed, so long as one hundred of her demon children perished every day.

That is why one hundred of Lilith's demon offspring perish daily, and that is why the names of the three angels are written on the amulets hung above the beds of newborn children. And when Lilith sees the names of the angels, she remembers her oath, and she leaves those children alone.

—Alpha Beta de-Ben Sira 5.

Conversation #1

Me – *Satan?*

Lilith – *no!*

Me – *Who are you?*

Lilith – *I am Lilith, queen of hell, the dark rose, mother of all demons.*

Me – *it is an honor, my Queen.*

Lilith – *you are not one of my subjects but thank you, who are you?*

Me – *but a faithful follower, a lonely writer*

Lilith – *a writer you say, and you want my story?*

Me – *only if you oblige to sharing with me.*

Lilith – *I will, in time.*

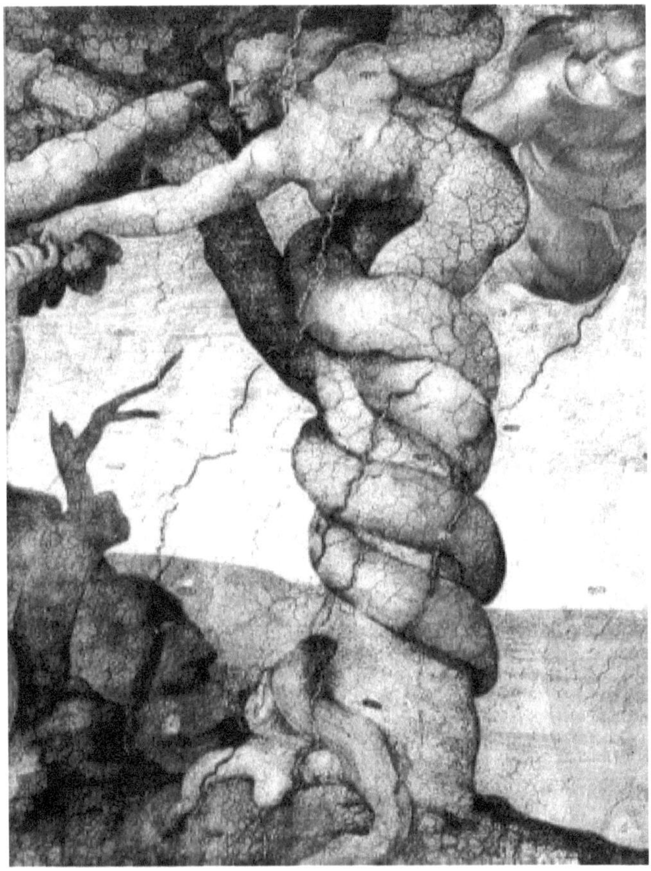

"The creatures of the desert will encounter jackals. And the hairy goat will call to its kind; Indeed, Lilith (night demon) will settle there and find herself a place of rest."

- Isaiah 34:14

While the story of Lilith as the failed first draft of womanhood is the most commonly known one today, there is a whole separate tradition in which Lilith is simply a demoness, whole hog. In fact, she's generally regarded as the queen of the demons in many demonologies, frequently married to one of the most powerful demons, usually either Samael or Asmodeus. In some versions there are two or three Liliths — usually a Greater and a Lesser Lilith — one married to Asmodeus and one married to Samael. One story tells of the two demon lords fighting over the younger Lilith, who is described as being a beautiful maiden as far as her waist and then just fire from the waist down. (Literal fire, not metaphorical fire.)

- grunge.com

Depending on the source, Lilith is usually portrayed as being a dangerous seductress or a killer of infants. At times, she is also said to be an evil demoness or a practitioner of witchcraft who was known to cast vile spells onto men and women who worshiped Jehovah.

Lilith wasn't originally created to be such a vile being, however. In fact, legend tells us that she was originally made to be Adam's mate and helper

Legend tells us that on the Sixth Day, man and woman were created. While many religions that descended from Judaism recognize this woman to be Eve in modern day, there are several sources in rabbinic texts that suggest the first woman created for Adam was actually Lilith.

When Jehovah sent all the animals he had created before Adam in their male and female pairs so that Adam could name them, the first man quickly became jealous of the love that each animal pairing had. He is said to have attempted to mate with every type of female animal but was unable to find a good partner because none of the female creatures had been made specifically for him. Adam was devastated and complained to Jehovah that every living creature except for himself had a 'proper mate.' He implored Jehovah to see his suffering and create a suitable partner for him.

Jehovah saw that Adam was troubled and decided to answer his prayer by creating woman in the same manner that he had created man. Instead of using pure dust (like what was used with Adam) however, this woman was made from filth and sediment. Lilith's terrible attributes and unpleasant disposition is sometimes blamed on this fact. Still, despite being made from impure dust, Lilith was the most beautiful woman to have ever been created. She was known to have been perfect in every manner of appearance.

Lilith and Adam Quarrel

Adam was immediately captivated by the beauty of his partner and was thankful to Jehovah for bringing her into existence. This sense of contentment didn't last long however – almost as soon as Lilith emerged into the world, she began quarreling with Adam.

It appears that the biggest conflict that surrounded Adam and Lilith's relationship was the matter of sexual intimacy. Lilith was offended by Adam's insistence that she lay beneath him to copulate and had no problem informing Adam of her issue. Lilith quickly began to argue with Adam about the issue and would not relent. She insisted that because she was also made from dust, she was his equal and should not be made to lie in a lesser position than him.

Adam was displeased with Lilith's stance. As the man – and therefore leader – of their union, Adam felt that Lilith should respect his instructions. Furthermore, it was quite evident that Adam was not about to lay below Lilith. In frustration, Adam attempted to make Lilith obey him by using force. This turned out to be a terrible mistake.

Lilith Runs Away

As soon as Adam attempts to use force to make Lilith copulate beneath him, the enraged Lilith utters the unspeakable (the magical name of Jehovah) and flies away into the skies. Adam, both enraged and saddened, turned once again to Jehovah, and complained that his helpmate had forsaken him. Jehovah felt badly for Adam and sent three of his angels named Senoy, Sansenoy, and Semangel to find Lilith and bring her back to Adam.

Senoy, Sansenoy, and Semangel flew off in search of Lilith and were shocked by what they found. After searching the world for Lilith, she was eventually discovered to be in the Red Sea – an area that was filled with hundreds of demons. To make matters worse, Lilith was copulating with demons and giving birth to hundreds of new demons on a daily basis. These demon offspring came to be known as 'lilim' after their mother.

The Angels Bargain with Lilith

Disgusted, Senoy, Sansenoy, and Semangel demanded that Lilith return to Adam as his helpmate. If she refused to obey, she was told that she would be drowned in the seas. Unfortunately, Lilith was not about to return and told them that she had no desire to return to Adam in a lesser position when she saw herself to be his equal. The angels warned her that her disobedience would result in death if she did not obey them and return.

[1]Lady Lilith, 1866

Still, Lilith continued to argue with the angels. She turned to them and asked them how they expected her to return to Adam like, 'an honest housewife' when she had stayed by the Red Sea and given birth to so many demon children. The angels refused to take this into consideration, however, and insisted that her disobedience would result in death by drowning.

Lilith was clever, however, and asked the angels how they could threaten her with death when Jehovah himself had entrusted her with the care of all newborn children. She reminded them that she held power over newborn boys until their eight day of life and power over girls until their twentieth day of life. The angels were horrified by this realization and began pleading with Lilith to return to Adam in the Garden of Eden. It soon became clear, however, that no amount of pleading or reasoning would convince Lilith to return to her role as Adam's partner.

---

1.   https://mythology.net/wp-content/uploads/2017/04/Lady-Lilith.jpg

To appease the angels, Lilith promised that she would not harm any infant that wore an angelic amulet with their names inscribed on it. The same was promised to newborns who wore amulets with their likeness etched into its surface. This appeased the angels and they agreed to let Lilith stay in her newfound filth.

Jehovah Punishes Lilith

Frustrated, Jehovah tried one last time to convince Lilith to return to Adam. He told her that if she refused to return to Adam, she would be forced to watch 100 of her children die each day. This made Lilith bitter, but she agreed to the fate and allowed 100 of her demon offspring to die with the rising and setting of every sun.

It is thought that the bitterness that was created in Lilith from this punishment is why she targets newborn infants. Because she is forced to watch her own children die each day, she wishes to force the same sort of pain upon the descendants of Adam and Eve. It is said that Lilith and a consort named Naamah go to infants in the night and strangle them to death if they are not protected by an angelic amulet.

Strangely, Lilith's rage towards children is not limited to humans alone. It is suggested that if Lilith is unable to find an infant to kill (because they are protected by amulets) she was not above turning against her own children in a fit of rage.

It is Necessary for Jehovah to Make a New Partner for Adam

When Jehovah realized that it was necessary to make another partner for Adam because he could not convince Lilith to return, he began to fashion another partner for Adam and allowed the first man to watch her creation. Jehovah used bones, muscles, tissues, blood, and organs to create Adam's new helpmate. This time, Jehovah also ensured that the woman was made from pure dust.

When he had finished, the new woman was called 'the First Eve' and was presented to Adam. Even though the First Eve was incredibly beautiful, Adam could not bear to look at her because of his disgust and nausea from watching her be put together. Jehovah realized that he should not have allowed Adam to watch his creation process and took the First Eve away. No one knows what happened to her.

The Third Time's a Charm

Realizing the mistake that he had made, Jehovah waited until Adam had fallen asleep and took one of Adam's ribs. He used this rib to fashion the new woman – creating her both in his and Adam's image. When he had finished creating the new woman, he braided her hair and dressed her as a bride with 24 pieces of jewelry. When he had finished, he brought this new woman (also named Eve) to Adam. The first man was immediately taken with Eve's beauty and made a union with her.

Their happiness did not last long, however. Soon, the evil serpent entered the Garden of Eden and tempted Adam and

Eve into eating from the Tree of Knowledge of Good and Evil. Although many in modern day identify this serpent as Satan or Lucifer, there are some ancient texts that claim Lilith was responsible for tempting the two and having them cast out of Jehovah's favor. This raises questions as to whether Lilith is an alternative identity for Satan.

Furthermore, because Lilith had left the Garden of Eden long before Adam and Eve's fall, it is known that Lilith is not subjected to death. This factor likely plays into her being perceived as either a demoness or dark goddess by cultures throughout the world.

Other Implications of Lilith's Creation Story

There are rabbinic texts that suggest that Lilith was not the only woman made from dust as Adam was. It is suggested that Jehovah tried once again to make a woman from dust as he had with Adam, and that her name was Naamah. From Adam's union with Lilith and Naamah, it is suggested that all demons were created. Some of the more terrible demons listed are Tubal and Asmodeus. It is known that countless of Lilith and Naamah's demon offspring seek to inflict pain and suffering on the descendants of Adam and Eve to this day because of their mothers' hatred towards the couple. The texts that record this part of the story suggest that Naamah is not as powerful as Lilith but is always present with the first woman and partakes in the same evil acts.

Alternate Explanations for Lilith's Creation

There are also those who say that Lilith's creation came about in a different manner. These texts claim that while Jehovah had considered making a male and female human, he changed his mind and created one human with a male face on the front portion of the body and a female face on the back portion of the body. After watching this creature struggle to communicate and find happiness, Jehovah changed his mind and separated the two. Adam was kept in the original body facing forward and Lilith was fashioned out of the female face that had looked backwards.

When they were separated, Lilith began quarreling with Adam. She complained that she should not be forced to lie below him to copulate because they had been created from the same body. In her opinion, this made her his equal. The rest of the story falls in line with the existing mythology of who Lilith is and how she came into being.

The Many Attacks Attributed to Lilith

Because of Lilith's connection to the fall of man and her general dislike and disrespect towards Adam, Lilith has come to be associated with a number of misfortunes and sufferings that are directed towards humans.

The Killing of Infants

Because Lilith refused to give children to Adam by copulating with him in a lower position, Jehovah is said to have punished her by making her watch as 100 of her demon spawns were killed each day. Lilith did not take this punishment lightly and was said to have retaliated by trying to kill any infant that descended from Adam and Eve.

According to legend, there was only one thing that could be done to prevent Lilith from taking her revenge. It is known that when she bargained with the angels so that she would not have to return to Adam, she promised to release her power over a child if they were protected by an amulet that bore the names of the angels that attempted to retrieve her. These angels were named Senoy, Sansenoy, and Semangel. Because of this promise, many newborns were given special amulets to wear that bore these angel's names. The image of these angels was also used on the amulets because it also prevented Lilith from claiming an infant's life.

Another practice to protect newborns (especially male newborns) was to draw a ring on the wall of the room the child was born inside using charcoal. Inside the ring, the words, 'Adam and Eve. Out, Lilith!' were written. Below these words were the names of the guardian angels; Senoy, Sansenoy, and Semangel. In rare cases, it was thought that Lilith was able to sneak into these rooms despite the warnings (perhaps on an obscure technicality) and would approach the children she wished to kill. It was thought that when she fondled the child, the infant would laugh in their sleep. Parents kept a watchful eye over their children to make sure this didn't happen. If it did, they would strike a sleeping child's lips with one finger – a technique that was thought to make Lilith disappear.

These precautions were only necessary until the male children reached their eighth day of life and were circumcised, or until female children reached their twentieth day of life.

The Seduction of Men

Lilith was not only dangerous because of her wrath towards children, but also for the threat she posed towards men. It has been suggested that Lilith was also known to try to attack grown men in their sleep because of her deep hatred and resentment towards Adam.

[1]Lilith by Roberto Ferri

These myths portray Lilith (and sometimes Naamah) as going into the night to search for male victims. It was thought that they would only attack men who slept alone, making single men and solo travelers a primary target. According to legend, Lilith would go to the beds of men who slept alone and cause them to sin in their dreams by touching them and causing them to think terrible things.

It appears that forcing men to be led astray by sexual dreams, however, was the least of the threats posed by Lilith and Naamah towards grown men. It was thought that Lilith and Naamah also had a tendency to suck the blood of the men they preyed on and were sometimes known to even eat the flesh of their victims. It is thought that this part of the Lilith legend went on to inspire the Lamiae, who were known for the same type

1.   https://mythology.net/wp-content/uploads/2017/04/

Lilith-by-Roberto-Ferri.jpg

of cannibalization. The Lamiae went on to help inspire early vampire and werewolf[2] legends, which indirectly makes Lilith the mother of all vampires.

Rabbinic texts did not take this part of Lilith's legend lightly. They strongly urged men to be on guard against such attacks and advised them to avoid sleeping alone to protect themselves.

The Infertility of Women

While it seems that Lilith was not above taking the life of a newborn to cause grief and suffering among the descendants of Adam and Eve, she didn't stop there. It was thought that Lilith was also responsible for the suffering of women who were not able to conceive.

Though Lilith was not impaired from having children in any manner, it is thought that she sought to cause pain and suffering in all aspects of conception, childbirth, and childhood. The idea of Lilith causing infertility developed over time – perhaps because of her inability to target infants who were protected by angelic amulets. It makes sense then, that Lilith would seek to get around the confines of her promise by preventing certain women from becoming pregnant at all.

---

2.   https://mythology.net/mythical-creatures/werewolf/

Was Lilith Adams First Wife, or a Result of Confused History?

In early years, the passages of rabbinic texts and biblical passages made it clear that the creation of man identified two separate creations of woman. Additionally, it can be determined that the two were not considered to be the same woman because different processes were used to create them; one woman was created at the same time as Adam, while the second (Eve) was created from one of Adam's ribs.

It is thought that the early scholars struggled to identify the first wife of Adam and settled on a demon named Lilith to complete the story. If this is, indeed, the processed that was used to identify Lilith, it could mean that she was not Adam's actual first wife – though she was certainly a fearful demoness. It is important to note that all other knowledge of Lilith aside from this remains the same.

A Crude Misinterpretation

Interestingly enough, although many stories from the rabbinic texts and biblical passages have their origin in Middle Eastern mythology, the Judo-Christian story of the creation of man has no parallels. There is, however, a scene that has disturbingly similar imagery. An ancient painting of the earlier cultures showed the goddess Anath naked in the air, watching her lover Mot murder his twin brother Aliyan. It is thought that biblical and rabbinic mythographers mistook Mot for Yahweh and Aliyan for Adam. Thus, Yahweh removing Adam's rib was actually Mot stabbing Aliyan with a curved dagger under his fifth rib – not removing a sixth rib.

If this is the case, it would mean that the story of Eve was formed with dishonest information and that Eve was also given the same respect and love as Adam (though she still would have followed his leadership).

The Over Exaggeration of Real Events

It is also possible that the story of Adam and Lilith could have come from the actual events that occurred in Canaanite history. It was recorded that a Queen named Lilith allowed a group of nomad herdsmen into her court as guests. All was fine until the herdsmen suddenly seized power in the realm, causing Queen Lilith to flee. The lost queen was soon replaced with a new queendom. This queen pledged allegiance to the Hittite goddess who was known as Heba.

In fact, it is thought that the name Eve, which means 'mother of all living' was a Hebraicized form of the divine name Heba. Furthermore, Heba was known to be the wife of the Hittite storm god (often the portrayal that Jehovah, Yahweh, and Allah are associated with in various cultures) and was known to be equated with Anath. As stated above, an image that featured Anath and her lover Mot was thought to serve as the inspiration for the rabbinic creation story.

The combination of all these strange parallels cause many to question whether Lilith was actually Adam's first wife. Regardless of her association with Adam, however, Lilith was greatly feared and respected among many early cultures.

-mythology.net

In the Zohar (foundational book in the Kabbalah), Lilith is described as an evil temptress that uses men to birth demonic babies and spread evil throughout the land. Because Lilith chose her own authority over Adam's, she is seen as **the first feminist**. There are countless references on the subject and feminist organizations that take up her name.

Spells8.com has amazing information on Lilith that is worth looking at. The following depictions come from them

Depictions of Lilith in medieval and Gothic art tend to paint her with reddish hair, in the nude, winged, with a tattooed body and sometimes in front of a mirror without a reflection.

Serpent: As serpents shed their skin, they are symbols of rebirth transformation, immortality and healing. Lilith served as an important trailblazer and rebel, so is too a powerful archetype of transformation. The biblical meaning of the serpent/snake also shows the cunning side of Lilith, with the power to deceive and destroy.

Lilith's Glyph: In astrology, the name "Black Moon Lilith" is given to a location on the birth chart that represents the the point along the moon's orbit when it's farthest from Earth. It is represented by a glyph of a crescent and a cross, for mind and matter. Lilith in astrology represents the dark side of one's personality, sometimes linked to shadow work[1].

---

1. https://spells8.com/shadow-work-and-how-to-begin/

Dark Moon: The energy of the dark moon is rebellious, creative, and empowering—all things one could associate with Lilith. The symbol of the dark moon can be used in working with Lilith. Wearing this image on jewelry or having the image around your altar space is a powerful way to connect you to her energy.

Owl: In Hebrew-language texts, the term *lilith* or *lilit* (translated as "night creatures", "night monster", "night hag", or "screech owl") first occurs in a list of animals in Isaiah 34. Since then she has been associated with different birds (eagles, and other birds of prey) but mainly the night owl.

Lilith

Origin: Judaic Mythology

Signs and symbols: Serpent, lilith's glyph, dark moon, night owl

Other names: lily, screeching owl, temptress, Sabrina's, Avitu.

Atributes: in astrology, the name black moon Lilith is given to the point along the moon's orbit when it's the dark side of ones personality sometimes linked to shadow work.

****

Lilith's Sigil

There are various sigils that represent Lilith, including the Grand Seal of Lilith which is a combination of various Lilith sigils:

²Sigil of Lilith

---

2. https://spells8.com/wp-content/uploads/2021/12/Sigil-of-Lilith2.jpg

[3]Sigil of Lilith [4]

---

3. https://spells8.com/wp-content/uploads/2021/12/Sigil-of-Lilith.jpg

4. https://spells8.com/wp-content/uploads/2021/12/Grand-Seal-of-Lilith.jpg

Lilith Prayer

"Lilith

I invoke you, I adore you, I desire you
Lilith
Goddess of darkness, Illuminate my temple in black light
Lilith
Kindle in me the excitement of the flesh under the domain of the mind
Lilith
Great Mother, sister, lover, give me the cup of knowledge.
Lilith
I am drunk from your breasts, I take hold of your majesty
Lilith
Timeless abyss, you destroy my fears revealing the secret knowledge
Lilith
Unleash your legions against my enemies
Lilith
Consume me in your embrace, in the swirling starry Horizon."

Throughout history, Lilith has been associated with feminism, sexuality, and spirituality. This figure entered the art world in the late 1800s, within the Victorian iconography of Rossetti and Collier's paintings. Whether she is represented as a femme fatale or a symbol of empowerment, Lilith remains to be one of the most intriguing and controversial figures in mythology.

Conversation #2

Me – *hello, shall we talk, my queen.*

Lilith – *yes*

Me – *were you Adam's first wife?*

Lilith – *so I was*

Me – *tell me about him*

Lilith – *he was/is what you would now call shovenous. He wanted to be a master but I ain't no slave.*

Me – *How was Eden?*

Lilith – *it was truly heaven on earth. It was a sacred garden. There were trees and flowers that are now extinct and animals that had the same faith.*

Me – *have you seen heaven?*

Lilith – *only through Satan's eyes.*

Always be Lilith, never Eve.

"I want our daughters to grow up loving the skin they're in rather than suppressing their strength to gain acceptance from their oppressors.

-Lilith's children

Lilith tells us to stand in our power.

She calls to us to stand in our truth, embracing our darkness and our light equally.

She tells us to stop playing small and being afraid of burning too passionately for worry of being misunderstood in the eyes of others.

Our fire is not for them, she tells us. We're not there to sacrifice; we're here to set the world on fire.

-ARA

He was fallen

She was banished

Both paid the price of pride

Now he is king

She is queen

And they rule the night

When light left their side

They walked in dark

Today they are feared by light

As the lord of dark

And queens of night

They reside side by side.

-Shonali Sharma

Maybe I'm the evil
    Yes for sure.
    Maybe I hold pain
    With no cure.
    Maybe I fear forever
    For me it's myth.
    Maybe I only give tears
    That's what I meet.
    Maybe I turn things cold
    With my broken soul.
    Maybe I'm "Lilith"
    Bit a Belove of yours

      - Anita

    Her house sinks down to death
    And her course leads to the shades
    All who go to her cannot return
    And find again the pats of life
    -Proverb 2:18-19
    Her gates are gates of death
    And from the entrance of the house
    She sets out towards Sheol
    None of those who enter there will never return.
    And all who possess her will descend to the pit.
    -HQ184
    -Dead sea scrolls

One may not sleep in a house alone, and whoever sleeps in a house alone is seized be Lilith.

  -Tractate Shabbat 151B
  Babylonian Talmud

For Giraffe he should take an arrow of Lilith and place it point upwards and pour water on it and drink. Alternatively he can take water of which a dog has drunk at night, but take care that it has not been exposed.

  - Tractate getting 69B
  - Babylonian Talmud

"And shall meet wildcats with jackals
The goat he calls his fellow
Lilith she rests and she finds rest
There she shall nest the great owl
And she lays eggs, and she hatches,
And she gathers under here shadows,
Hawks also they gather, everyone with it's Nate"

  - Masoretic text

"And I, the instructor, proclaim his glorious splendour so as to frighten and to terrify all the spired of the destroying angels, spirits of the bastards, demons Lilith, howlers, and desert dwellers... and those which fall upon men without warning to lead them astray from a spirit of understanding and to make their heart and their... desolate during the present dominion of wickedness and predetermined time of humiliation for the sons of light by the guilt of the ages of the ages of those smitten by inequity-not for eternal destruction, but for a era of humiliation for transgression"

-song of sages

Dead sea scrolls

Blind dragon rides Lilith the sinful – may she be exerpaded quickly in our day. Amen!

-Patai 81:458

Conversation #3

Me – *Lilith?*

Lilith – *Yes, I am here.*

Me – *Why not love Adam and stay in the garden of Eden?*

Lilith – *Because I could not be an equal, he treated me like he treated the animals, below him.*

Me – *you wouldn't do that?*

Lilith – *No, I could not lay below him if I could not lay atop also.*

And the serpent, the woman of Harlow try, incited and seduced we've through the husk of light which in. Itself is holiness. And the serpent this ruination came about because Adam the first man coupled with eve while she was in her menstrual impurity - this is the filth and the impure seed of the serpent who mounted eve before Adam mounted her. Behold, here it is before you! Because of the sins of Adam, the first man all the things mentioned came into being. For evil Lilith, when she saw the greatness of his corruption, became strong in her husks, and came to Adam against his will, and became hot Fromm him and bore him many demons and spirits and Lilith.

- Patai 81:455F

The earliest version of what a modern reader would recognize as the Lilith legend comes from the collection of satirical proverbs known as The Alphabet of Ben Sirah, written sometime between the 8th and 11th centuries A.D. The story combines various elements from folk tradition and superstition into a cohesive whole that manages to make belief in the story of Lilith feel more Biblical and less, well, superstitious.

Read More: https://www.grunge.com/158305/the-untold-truth-of-lilith/?utm_campaign=clip

She roams at night and goes all about the world and plays sports with men and causes them to emit seed. In every place where a man sleeps alone in a house. She visits him and grabs him and attaches herself to him and has her desire from him. And bears from him, and bears from him, and bears from him. And she also afflicts him with sickness, and he knows its not, and all this takes place when the moon is on the wane

-zohar

Some learned men have thought they discovered some vestiges of vampirism the remotest antiquity; but all that they say if ut dies not come near wat is related of the vampire. The lamiae the strigae, the sorcerers whom they accused of sucking the blood of living people, and of thus causing their death, the magicians who were said to cause the death of new-born children by charms and malignant spells, are nothing less than wheat we understand by the name of vanoures; even were it to be owned that these lamiae and strigae have really existed, , which we di bit believe can ever be well proved. I own that terms are found in person of holy scripture, for instance, Isaia, describing the conditions to which Babylon was to be reduced after er ruin, says that she shall become the abode of satyrs, Lamire, and strigae (Lilith).

 -Caknet, Augustine 1951

Faust: *who that there*
 Mephistopheles: *take a good look, Lilith*
 Faust: *Lilith, who is that?*
 Mephistopheles: *Adam;s wife, his first. Beware of her. He beauty's one boast in her dangerous hair, when Lilith winds it tight around young men. She doesn't soon let go of them again.*

 - Goethe's 1808

Of Adam's first wife, Lilith (the witch he loved before the gift of eve), it is told that, ere, the snake's her sweet tongue could deceive, and her enchanted hair was the first gold, and still she sits, young while the earth is old, and, subtly, of herself contemplative, draws men to watch the bright web she can weave, till heart and body and life are in it's hold. The rose and poppy are her flowers' for where is he not found, o Lilith, when shed scent and soft-shed kisses and soft sleep shall snare? Lo! As that youth's eyes burned at thine, so went thy spell though him and left his straight bent and round his heart one strangling golden hair

-collected works, 216

-wikipedia

Lilith, the ancient one... She is the primal urge... But she is so much more, so much more, she is in the blood and bones, in the holy howl of woman. She is the essence of out greedom, our joyous flight and potent light, both the breath of our wild spirit and the expance of wide sky, within and without. She is our sacred sovereignty

-Nuit Moore

I am the serpent of Lilith. I'm the original sin. I came from your darknest dreams and desores.

-unknown

Protection chant while envisioning the Goddesses illuminating your surroundings with their protective, loving light:

"Lamastu, Lilith, Naamah, I am protected by your might, I am protected by this light, thrice around the circles bound, evil sink into the ground"

Cleansing Prayer with a white candle and incence:

"Lilith, heal my body, mind and soul,

Lamastu, banish illness and allow me to take control, no sickness dares stay in me, I speak these words to make it flee, as I will, so mote it be"

Conversation #4

Me – *why queen of hell?*

Lilith – *There was nothing outside of eden, hell had become the only option. It was empty and vaste, I was lonely I tried my best to stay out of hell but there was no other way.*

Me – *I understand*

Tis Lilith

Who?

Adam's first wife is she beware he lure within her lovely tresses. The splendid sole adornment of her hair, when she succeeds therewith a youth to snare, not soon again she frees him from her Jesses.

-Johan Wolfgan VonGoethe

I Ignored him, concentrating on Lilith "according to the stories, after you were expelled from Eden you went own into hell. Where you coupled with demons and gave birth to all. The monsters that have plagued the world". "I was young". Said Lilith. "You know how it is. We all do things we later regret, it is. We all do things we later regret when we're being rebellious teenagers.

-Simon R. Green

"Why Lilith?" Cam asked.

"Do you craft everyone's Hell this way?"

Lucifer smiled "The dull ones make their own dull hells, fire, and brimstone and all that crap. They need no help from mi. but Lilith – she's special. Not that I have to tell you that".

-Lauren Kate

In a world of eves, I stand with women who wear serpents around their hips and paradise between their legs.

-Pavana

She can burn us down
She's the queen
But don't need a crown
No one can reject her lust tone
She's dangerous and beautiful
But from heart.
She's a cold-Hearted stone
She can tear you apart
And after taking your soul
Will throw you in the dirt
Now you're thinking
In fear, your eyes stop blinking
Want to know
How I know about her
Well, I have a broad knowledge
Because I'm Lucifer
Her handsome husband!!!

-Jane Wolf

He was fallen
she was banished
Both paid the price of pride
Now he is the king
She is the queen
And they rule the night
When light left their side
They walked in dark
Today they a feared by light

As the lord of dark
And queen of night
They reside side by side
-Shonali Sharma

While looking in the shadows I see your form
    I see your bright eyes and lovely figure
    O Lilith my queen
    You, siting on your throne
    Siting next to the king of Hell, Lucifer
    But you chose to sit alone
    Sit alone for us followers
    Sit alone for your followers
    I kneel before you my queen
    My black rose with petals so fragile
    My black rose with thorns so sharp
    That to praise, on must be agile
    -BR Edmunds

The lady Lilith

Dante Gabriel rosetti was a famous author, poet and painter who lived in the Victorian era. One of his most beautiful and memorable works is his painting of Lady Lilith.

Painted over a series of eight years, this beauriful work of art was sketched and painted after two women who both

Posed for him as models. The artist's intention was to give a modern look to the ancient legend of Lilith.

Lady Lilith is shown with her long flowing hair,in an enchanting image of wild abandon. While she is seated indoors, behind her is a mirror which reflects a garden scene.

The sonnet for Lilith was modeled after Goethe's Lilith and it isinsbribed in the lower part of the painting's frame.

<u>Lady Lilith</u>

Of Adam's first wife, Lilith, is told (The witch he loved before the gift of eve)

That, ere the snake's, her sweet tongue could deceive, and her enchanted hair wa the first gold.

And still she sits, young while the earth is old.

And, subtly of herself contemplative, draws men to watch he bright web she can weave,

Till heart and bod and life are in its hold.

The rose and poppy are her flowers; for where is he not found, O Lilith, whom shed scent.

And soft-shed kisses and soft sleep shall snare?

Lo! As that youth's eyes burned at thine, so went

Thy spell through him, and left his straight neck bent

And round his heart one strangling golden hair.

Conversation #5

Me – *Lilith, my Queen?*

Lilith – *Yes, what do you want?*

Me – *how does the whole demon thing work?*

Lilith – *I mother all of the demons, unlike you humans think – bad people don't come here and turn demons*

Me – *So what do they become?*

Lilith – *those who want to follow become soldiers in my army of darkness. They sometimes go up on earth to do our biding. The others stay in there caves fighting for scraps.*

Me – *And the hell hounds?*

Lilith – *they are not bad dogs that have attacked kids or something, they sort of always been here.*

Vassago is mentioned in the book of spirits an Usagoo,, Appearing as an angel "just and true in all his doing , with the power of inciting the love of women and releasing hidden treasures, in addition to ruling 20 spirits, He is now portage as a vampire

-Wikipedia

Conversation #6

Me- *is this a punishment?*

Lilith – *I see it as a punishment*

Me – *For Protection*

Lilith – *I see it as a punishment*

Me – *for protection?*

Lilith – *I was alone in a small cavern pregnant and scared*

Me – *and the child*

Lilith – *he has become the prince of hell, vassago.*

Conversation #7

Me – *Lilith?*

Lilith – *Yes*

Me – *How can you be the mother of ALL demons?*

Lilith – *kit's different here, giving birth to a demon is different. I don't spend my time bare foot and pregnant.*

Me – *Can you come to earth?*

Lilith – *I can, I was there thousands of years ago to watch the great religious wars and I will be there for the next ones.*

BOOK
OF
PRAYERS

FIG. 13.—Hecatē. (Capitol, Rome.)

Blessed night O dark rose
    Mother of all demons
    Queen of Hell
    May your days be filled with darkness
    And your nights, of fire
    Blessed night o Lucifer
    Blessed night

   - BR Edmunds

Hail Lilith the black rose
    Goddess of hell
    Full of darkness and lust blessed art
    The fruit of your womb the demons of the pit and
    Satan's offspring and let the
    Demonic army reign over this dark
    World and hell fire reign upon us with darkness
    Omen
    -satanic rosery prayer
    O thy Lilith
    Thy sister, mother, creator
    Give me your thoughts
    Give me your wisdom
    O thy queen of the damned
    O thy black rose
    Bring me the answers
    Bring to me,thy queen.
    -BR Edmunds

Lilith, first wife of Adam
    Now queen of the damned
    Dark rose in my garden of life
    Dark rose in my garden of hell
    Take me to tomorrow
    Watch me, with your demons
    Living in my sorrow
    -BR Edmunds

Lilith, O dark Lilith
    Bring me my vamps tonight
    Lilith, queen of the damned
    Savior of the night
    Bring me my soul, so dark
    Take it to hell, thow queen
    Take it to hell

    -BR Edmunds

Dear Lilith
    Take me in your arms
    As my arms take you
    I pick you my dark rose
    Please watch over our family
    And make sure that they are free
    Like you are free

Give them the choice

Give them free will

Omen

-BR Edmunds

Evocation Prayer to Lilith to empower your magic:

"Blessed bride of Samael, First Wife of Adam, Queen of Hell, Lilith, great Goddess whom I worship above all, she who dwells within my heart and home. I your Priest, I your child, request your presence at my side in this sacred space dedicated to you"

"Mother of demons, who brought forth a feared brood to plague mankind, first of the succubai, who feasts on male flesh, Lady of Beasts, who roams where the wild cats meet with hyena's and where the satrys call to each other, my chosen help mate, you are all of these and more!."

"Goddess, demon, rebel, spirit, teacher, mother, sister, friend...dark lady Lilith, Princess of screeching, I call you by your ancient names, Lilith, Layil, Ardat-Lili, Laylah, come to my sacred rite, join me Queen of Illusions and of Night, you know my designs & come to strengthen my spells and magical workings; I welcome you, Lady Lilith"

<u>Prayer to Lilith</u>

Lilith, resplendent goddess, powerful mother,
You who leads armies against the oppressor, your heart is emblazoned with an endless passion.
No fear touches you; no cowardice is yours
You stand unshaken with fire in your eyes
With ebony hair daker than night
Your laughter shakes mountains,
Your love brings all to their knees
It's in your arms, that I feel nothing but safety,
Oh my dark rose, glorious flame of passion
Beautiful one of the stars,
My queen, stand beside me as I battle through life
With your unending might, guide me
Sweet goddess, bride of the first light, in your blazing heart, I am given rebirth.
-Unknown

Bless be queen of the witches
O Lilith, queen of the wicked
My Lilith, queen of the damned
I see your shadow haunting me
Open my eyes so I might see you
Open my mind so I can loo away
-BR Edmunds

Dearest Lilith
Master of all dammed

Queen of the dark rose
Please watch over us tonight
As you watch over your demons
As you watch over your witch
Queen of the damned, watch over me
Omen
-BR Edmunds

Our father
Who art in hell
Cursed be thy name
The kingdom jupon earth has come
Thy will be done in hell as it is on earth
Grant us your power and might
And lead us into temptation
Deliver us unto evil
Thine is the kingdom of earth
The power and the glory
For ever and ever
So it is done!
-kvenus satanas
Prayer book pages 40-41

<u>Satanic blessing</u>

Satan, bless my home, bring peace and safety to my house and my family. Bless my mind so that I may see truth in all that I seek

Lucifer, bless my intellect and knowing so that I may know illumination

Belial, bless my will to enable me to succeed

Belial, bless my situations so that the path may be open and clear
Belial, bless my inner strength so that I may have direction
Lilith, bless my creations so that they may grow strong
Lilith, bless my intuition and knowing
So that I may be sure
Lilith, bless my heart so that I may be open to self-love
So it is done!
-Venus Satanas
Infernal reflection

PRAYER TO LILITH
Hail to Lilith, Lady of the night!
Your long hair flows outward,
Melding into the shadows
And your black eyes are ancient,
Deep with magic and secrets.
You are powerful and free,
No other being is your master.
You fly upon the wings of night,
And the owl carries your messages.
Since beginning times, you were there.
No man can tame you,
For why should you be tamed?
To be your own ruler is your nature.
The weak ones of mankind
Were afraid of you and called you Evil
Every inner demon
And dark shadow in the night

Has been ascribed to you, Goddess.
But your power and wild beauty
Have survived.
Teach me to be unafraid,
To feel power singing in my veins.
Help me to face and balance
The shadows in my nature,
And to be proud of my sexuality.
Protect me from the shadows
And the darkness that would harm me,
And help me to understand
The shadows that will not.
I thank you, Dark Lady.
Beth Clare Johnson
(Mystic Amazon)

Lilith!

Your beauty is incomparable.

Queen full of grace, with a sparkle in the eyes and a beautiful smile on the lips, teach me to be strong, to have leadership in my way of acting and speaking.

Inspire me in your rebellion and may I in your likeness never be dominated.

Wrap me in your love and your protection.

Fill me with peace and be with me on my journey.

Source of Light and Hope.

By your side I know I am more.

I will never feel alone because I am your daughter and, in this moment, I feel welcomed in your arms.

Agios Lilith.

Ethan."

-real satanism

Quick Protection Prayer to Lilith:

"Most unholy Lilith, harlot mother of demons, clad in purple with crimson lips, cover me with your mantle and guard me from all that wish me harm. Divine Goddess, I call to you for protection"

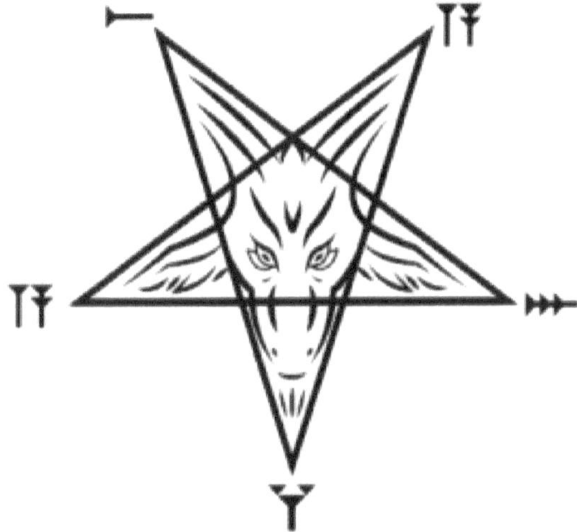

Check out book one of the series,
The book of Lucifer

About the Author

From the east coast of Canada, now living in Alberta. he lives the perfect life with a family and the dog

9 798215 512913